About the Author

Nick is a retired Learning Manager of English, Art, History, Life Skills and Learning Skills. He was also a Year Head and Manager of The Learning Resource Centre.

His feelings for WW1 grew through his attachment to his maternal Grandfather Sidney Bushell. 'Syd' was from Birmingham and before the war was, - 'Birmingham's Premiere Versatile Entertainer',- Syd Blackshields.

He joined the RGA as a trench mortar man. He fought on the Somme with the 38th Welch Division at Mametz Wood - and at Passchendaele. He won the MM & Bar for bravery. He was wounded and never fought again.

Nick lives in Sandwich, Kent and is involved with many creative activities. He is also 'horizonimage Art Photography'.

Dedication

This book of poems written by Nick Matthews is dedicated to his Great Uncle, Private Albert. T. Bushell, killed two days in the line. He was killed on 27:4:1918 between 12.00 and 2.00pm. He was Nick's maternal grandfather's younger brother. Albert was the youngest of nine. He was small and gentle, a delicate and artistic choir boy. Not a man for war. He worshiped Nick's grandfather who was with the RGA and who won the MM & Bar on the Somme and at Passchendaele.

Comparing the beauty of the Somme now with the horror 100 years ago.

The dedication was written in 1988 by John Giles who founded the Western Front Association (Nov 1980) www.westernfrontassociation.com

John lived near Nick in Ash, (Canterbury) Kent. He died in 1991.

Written by John Giles (now deceased)
author of –
'The Somme Then and Now,' 'Flanders Then and Now'
and
'The Western Front Then and Now'.

I am privileged to be asked to write a dedication to Private Albert T Bushell, 29688 Signaller, Grenadier Guards, 3rd Battalion, who died in the service of his country during the Great War and whose remains lie in one of the beautifully kept British military cemeteries in Northern France. Douchy-les-Ayette.

He was one of those fine young men who, far from being war-like or aggressive followed the example of others, joined the army, and after two days in the line was killed doing his duty.

It is right that the memory of this young soldier, and all those of that era who did not return home, should be kept green; they deserve to be remembered for all time. By preparing this book of poems, his great nephew, Nick Matthews, is helping to preserve that cherished memory and in doing so helps to ensure that others do not forget the sacrifices of those who 'gave their all' during the dark days of 1914-1918.

John Giles

Nick Matthews

WHEN WILL WE EVER LEARN?

AUSTIN MACAULEY
PUBLISHERS LTD.

A CIP catalogue record for this title is available from the British Library.

ISBN 9781785540400 (Paperback)
ISBN 9781785540417 (Hardback)

www.austinmacauley.com

First Published (2015)
Austin Macauley Publishers Ltd.
25 Canada Square
Canary Wharf
London
E14 5LQ

Printed and bound in Great Britain

Acknowledgments

Many, many thanks to:

Photography
Simon Matthews. libranstealphotography.co.uk
Dave Batchelor. Photography.
Nick Matthews. horizonimage@talktalk.net

Artists
Bob Martin MBE.
Julia Baxter

Calligraphy
Julia Baxter

Help, Support and Advice
Joy Matthews (my wife)
Kaye Matthews (my mother, Sid's younger daughter)

Prayer of Despair

Is it any different now?

I watched your body disintegrate,
acid soaked, radiated, burnt in horror
of what seemed ages, yet passed in seconds.
I saw your spirit pass
into the vast eternity of time,
your soul cried out, your voice rang clear
in agonising screams to hear.

Charred calcium, bright radium
great dust bowl, glassy stadium
wherein to act the death of millions,
the death of millions, the death of millions.

The sight, a falling point of shadow
far away above the lit metropolis;
it did not touch or reach the Earth.
An endless stream of atoms giving birth
to endless streams of atoms giving life
to endless streams of atoms, rising,
fuming up, a column, mushroom cloud…
With which you are familiar
with which, perhaps, you're proud.

Nick at the grave of Lieutenant Colonel John McCrae,
famous for his poem, - "In Flanders Fields".
(Wimereux/Boulogne France)

Trapped in a Trench
Below the 'Danger Tree'.
Newfoundland Memorial Park.
Somme.

Stretching up to touch that tree
Straining eyes, I *had* to see,
Leaves float down and small twigs break,
Falling back I lay awake.

Reaching out my left hand slipped,
Damp smooth stone, the rest was chipped,
Down below the quagmire slid
Once again a desperate bid.

Right hand up to reach the bar
That I had not seen so far,
Rust and splinters ripped my hand,
Grit fell off and turned to sand.

Why is that tree so high and far?
Why is that stone so smooth with tar?
Why does that quagmire turn and flow?
Why is not that bar too low?

I'll tell you why, because you're tired,
Upside down and side by side,
Chained and gagged and roped up tight,
Soon I'm sure you'll die of fright.

Nick Matthews. horizonimage

Douchy-les-Ayette

(Where my Great Uncle, Albert Thomas Bushell is buried.
19 years old -2 days in the line!)

Between this village and Ayette
The line was held
Against the great attack.
Retreating to this point the Guards
Lost many men and filled the ranks
With soldiers not yet tested in the war.

Some lie in graves close to
The places where they died.
And here lies Albert.

We found his grave
As tears of rain
Dripped softly from
A leaden sky to cry
His nineteen years into
The soil of France.

And taking photos of the place
With groups of stones,
Or his alone,
For those who couldn't come
We laid a plaque.

About him were five other men
Who died that day...
All dead... so many years ago.

Private Albert Thomas Bushell.
(Signaller Grenadier Guards)
Killed in action at Ayette, France.
Two days in the line
April 27th, 1918
Aged 19 years.

When Will We Ever Learn?

Throughout history we touch the door
and find us nothing, except war.
We never learn or see all in our hearts
But slaughter on and play the parts.

Why cannot we just see the pointless vain?
And cancel out the senseless pain
That only sends us into endless memories
Of young lost souls and lives that would have been.

Out on the Somme the great commanders didn't know
What had been done or where it all would go.
They used the cannon fodder time and time again
To wrench the hearts and total up the pain!

On July One they said to walk into the lines of death
But didn't know the enemy had taken breath,
And there across the softened lands
The innocents just died in bands.

Oh why, oh why did humans just not know
How war and battles would not show?
All lost lives were all lost lives of generations gone
And they can't hug the soul of just their little one.

They couldn't hug, they couldn't love
They couldn't work or worship all above.
They couldn't marry, hold her close,
They couldn't live, and that was worse.

When will we ever learn? When will we see
That War is simply not to be?

Look at all the history and total up the pain
That never makes the world more sane…

Nick Matthews
The grave of his Great Uncle Albert T Bushell

Dawn in Albert

Somme Picardy

I couldn't sleep that night.
The warmth that promised early
Morning mist mixed gently in my mind.
By two o'clock I felt that I'd absorbed
The souls of all the thousands dead
Across the Somme.

By six, the dawn had drawn
Down that moistened shroud and
Wrapped me in my furtive amble to
The outskirts of the town.

And there, surrounded by the crosses
Of the dead, "*Mort Pour la France*"
I stepped apon the chalky death we call
The Somme.

Silence.

Looking East and hopeful of some sun
As many soldiers once had done,
I gazed into the iridescent mist
And looked for ghosts of armies
Long since gone.

When leaning on the dark stone wall,
The boundary of many sufferings,
I knew what *they* had seen
When searching for an enemy...
Stand to!

Nick Matthews, *horizonimage*

Delville Wood

At Delville Wood South Africa lost many men
Who still line up in ranks as if to try anew
The brave assault upon the shattered place.
Three thousand entered through the trees
One forty came back out.
Now lying in their graves the stones
Stand without a doubt
To touch us with that holocaust
In 'Devil's Wood' we see.
The trees stand strong as soldiers did
Before the whole brigade was gone
And will forever make a bid
To feel the hurt on everyone.

We stopped there on our visit to the Somme
And in the cool of well provided shade
Could not believe what had been done.

At Delville Wood South Africa lost many men
Who still line up.

Nick Matthews, *horizonimage*

Somme….. ber

Gone are the moments of a torrid time
That bathed the Somme in richest agonies
And young men's cries that only serve to mime
The dreadful wickedness of naïve lies.

Now, in the residue of blooded iron
And the hearts of those that stayed at home
And in the stark accounts that we rely on,
Live the memories we cannot understand.

But in the abstract of so many years
There is a fine reality that stays
In rows of stones and monuments to fears
All born in stagnant trenches and in bays.

Across the Somme they hold a line of time
In rows of white
On deep grained chalk and ageing lime.

Nick Matthews, *horizonimage*

Touch the Reality
Beaumont Hamel

How rural, small and cosy
Lies this hamlet in the
Soul of Picardy, with
Narrow lanes and tracks
To manage country matters.

On a road, quite steep,
With little room to turn,
And partly hidden by the bank
There stands a hut
And overgrown yard
Containing rusted relics
Of a hell so awful that
Survivors couldn't tell.

But every autumn and in spring
They harvest evil pieces
Of a time, so long ago,
To gather in secluded corners
Of this place.

For Beaumont Hamel
Was a fortress
Made of mud and endless
Rows of tangled spikes
That ninety eight years ago
Held out against
The men who died
And still line up
Outside the wire…

Nick Matthews, *horizonimage*

Nick Matthews, *horizonimage*

Grandpa Sidney Bushell (Syd Blackshield - 'Birmingham's Premier Versatile Entertainer')

Acting Bombardier Sidney BUSHELL 60158 R.G.A.
MM & Bar
Attd. "X"/38 Trench Mortar Battery.

Fought on the Somme July 1916 attached to the
38th Welch Division and at Passchendaele.

I take after you…
You were a great performer
In Birmingham those days
And joked and played and juggled
To the audience in ways.
You were so very arty and danced
In entertaining,
The jokes were always funny
And totally pertaining,
To the age you lived in then.

You were a total 'Nutter' when you fought out on the Somme
You won the MM bravely and you really were 'the one',
You won the medal once again in Belgium the next year
And then were injured badly as the Germans got too near.
You never were the same again and never did perform,
Just grew your flowers gently
And was saddened in the dawn.

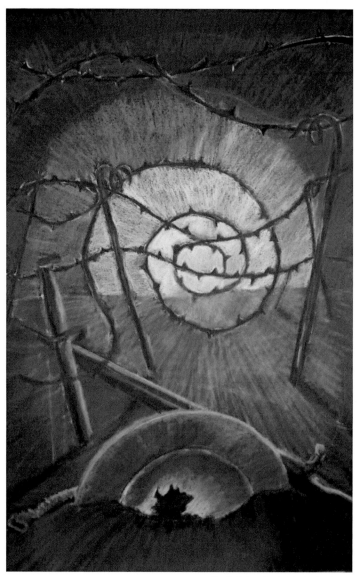

Bob Martin MBE. Artist

Beaumont Hamel

Here, we see it is not over
'Cross the shell holed lands,
Lines of trenches face each other
Where we see the bands…
See the bands of posts and wires
Running to the East.
Crossing fields of living hell still, it has not ceased.
See the signs that warn of death,
Death that could be now,
Unexploded shells lie waiting,
Do we know just how?
Ask the 'Death Tree', - "Was it true?"
Ask the 'Death Tree' more.
Ask the 'Death Tree,' - "Was it you?
Or shells and blood and gore?"

Little Ones

Enlisting for the Army role
Not knowing what the toll
Would be in total warfare,
Stood the line of younger teens.

They didn't know another
Smartened up and fully clothed
In their old day this was really good,
And now seemed just like those.

But under age and innocent
Recruiting sergeants should
Refuse their stand and understand
The devastating loss.

They did not want to know or care
If he was seventeen. They did not share
Or want to see if he was much too young.
At fifteen then, he looked okay
To just dress up and say-
"Yes Sir I'll do my duty right",
He's set off for the fray.
Under age and under flag the unit
Thought he ought to,
Just another soldier boy
To send into the slaughter!

Etaples

Here they trained with strictest stride
The thousands for the trenches,
Out upon the estuary in wildest northern weather
Marched the youngest raw recruits
To size up for endeavour,
Never knowing what's to come
But many came back,- never!

Here they healed so many souls
In hospitals so great.
But there were many not to help
Who suffered at the gate.
Just look at all the whitened stones
That line the local fields
And try to feel the suffering
That war and hate reveals.

Etaples lies soft and mellow now
Beneath the setting sun
And in our hearts we treasure them
Those thousands, every one.
The harshest training and the care
Was only just for war
Let's see it clear and know for us
Just no more…any more.

Albert Thomas Bushell.   Killed 2 days in the line

THE SOURCE IS SILENT NOW THE DAY HAS GONE,
THE LEAVES ARE BROWNER IN THE EVENING SUN,
THE NIGHT IS DEAD IN DRIPPING GOLD,
THE VAST EXPANSE OF DARK, FOR SORROW SOLD.
MORNING BRINGS AT ONE O'CLOCK
THE WHITE-RUST HAZEY DRIFTING MIST
AND THROUGH THE TREES ACROSS THE MARSH
A SHAPELESS WEARY VISION..... DRIFTING ON;
AND THEN, BENEATH THE GLINT OF SILVER
IN THE MIST
A CIRCLE GOLD, A MANTLE WHITE
ONE RAM, QUITE SAD AND MAGIC.....BLACK!
BUT THERE OR THERE OR FAR AWAY
THE LONELY DAWN IN SILENCE STAYS,
THE COCK CROWS, HAILS THE MORNING SUN
AND OFF THEY RACE TILL DAY IS DONE,
BUT ONLY IN THE DAY THEY DIE,
AT NIGHT THE FLOATING FIGURES FLY
AS ARROWS PARTING WAVES ACROSS THE HAZE
LIKE DEMONS IN AN ENDLESS MAZE

THE BLACK FOREST

Artwork and calligraphy, Julia Baxter

Golden Madonna, Albert, Somme.
Nick Matthews, *horizonimage*

Sunset on the Somme

The sun reversed on up the sky
I saw it when the heart slid by,
It skipped the stormy cloud up front
But round the sky it had to shunt.

It coloured orange, purple hue,
A gold that sloped behind so true,
And like the red of bloody heart
The colours sifted, fell apart.

At one degree we call it dawn
At twenty one the name is morn',
And not far off we call it 'soon'
When ninety, or straight up, at noon.

And when it angles off the pole,
The tea is brewed, the four bells toll.
Then later on, all on one side we look and sing,
And stupidly we call it "even" - evening!

The Tank Bank.
Project to raise money in the UK during WW1

The 'Tank Bank' raised the cash to buy it
All those weapons made of steel,
Tanks to kill and guns to injure
Cannon fodder on the field.
Loads of money just for war
Killing sons to see no more,
Buying Bonds to pay for slaughter,
People had not seen the door.

Had they opened up the portal,
Seen their sons die needlessly,
Sent up slopes to all machine guns
Not allowed to duck and dive.
Never mind, the Tank Bank flourished,
Taking on the piles of cash
Never thinking of the soldiers
Sinking in the' horrored mash'.

They Don't Know What They're Doing

They don't know what they're doing
They don't know where they went
They don't know what to look for
And survival, heaven-sent.

They don't know what they're doing
For France was far away
And in their time the great events
Were just not on display.

They don't know what they're doing
It all was really new,
They went with hope and glory -
Returning? Just the few.

They don't know what they're doing
It all was just a dream
They hoped to be excited
But nothing, so it seemed.

They don't know what they're doing
There's no way that they should.
We'd hoped they hadn't done it
But we know that, hey, *we* would!

Simon Matthews. libranstealphotography.co.uk

Simon Matthews. libranstealphotography.co.uk

Lochnagar Crater

When in July the line advanced
At steady walking pace
The soldiers outside Albert
Headed up-slope to the place,
And knowing, - as they had been told,
That storm of shell had ruined all ahead,
They walked towards the village
And the crater on the hill.

At first there, all was looking well
But in ten minutes full,
Of bitter bullets from the guns
Which really were not gone.
The 34th Division died,
For one in eight had gone
For little gain and total pain
Lochnager Crater's son.

Photograph – Dave Batchelor

What I Feel

The decades do not make it fade across the mellow Somme
Where thousands died to keep us safe and free from everyone.
Wide pastures drift in greens and touch
Of breeze across the fertile landscape,
That here, just now, keeps all of us
Quite free and total mellow.

The decades do not make it fade across the softened Somme
Where white stones lie in thousands, by the bowing trees.
Look wide across the sunny drift that pictures all the sky
And just remember all the lads
That came here… just to die.

We see it now, we stay so safe,
The scene is just so lovely,
All the images of life just rest here
Looking soft.
Across the Somme there lies a scene
That once was 'Total Hell,'
And now the rolling greenery is
Tolling – like the bell.

The bell of nearby Albert that never has forgot
The dead and sad, just little ones,
Whose lives were never got!

Nick Matthews, *horizonimage*

Nick Matthews, *horizonimage*

So Close and Yet so Far

Three thousand yards apart they died
The only two Le Crens
Listed, died in this Great War,
Both gentle, fighting men.

They both were killed six days apart
Across the rolling Somme,
And neither knew each other,
Or where each one was from.

For Percy was from London town,
The regiment's from there.
But at High Wood, machine-gunned down,
And lost in deep despair.

Ernest, from New Zealand
Left family all behind
And just his grave shows just how brave
This soldier, sure, had been.

Percy's name looks out across
The mellow distant lands,
High Thiepval will hold his name
For ever in soft hands.

Ernest's stone stands tall and good
So proud amongst the thousands,
At the back of Warlencourt
Across the summer lands.

There they rest for ever
Enlisted on a par,
Bonded in endeavour
So close, and yet so far.

Simon Matthews. libranstealphotography.co.uk

Simon Matthews. libranstealphotography.co.uk

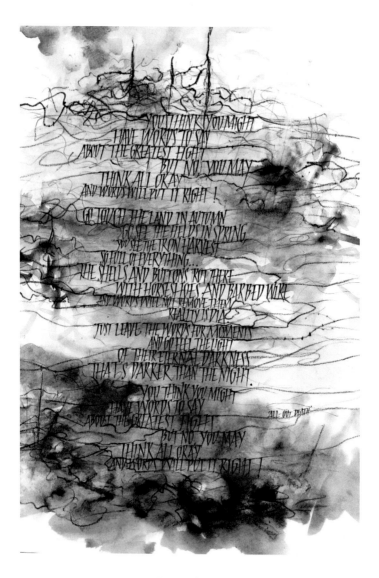

Artwork and calligraphy, Julia Baxter

Bob Martin MBE. Artist

Mametz

The haze, just parted,
Dissipated and so damp
Revealed the awesome darkness of the wood.

From such a distance
Dim it lay to herald out
The dead
With viscous whispers in its leaves.

Then closer, at the point
Where Welshmen died in
Bitter fighting for a foot hold in the
Stinging mouths of German guns,
I stood... I stood
Beside the fortress trees they call Mametz.

So in that place we breached
The undergrowth to stand amid the
Lofty sentinels of those long dead.

And there the wicked scars,
Scarce hidden by few fallen leaves,
Bore witness
To the battles many years before.

Then from within the gloom of 1916
We looked out to see the sun
Of modern days,
And there the ploughman turned
The soil in preparation of a bright tomorrow,
Throwing up metallic remnants
Of the slaughter years ago!

The Iron Harvest, Somme.

Fricourt

In their thousands, Germans died.
In the 'Death Shells' they were caught.
In their thousands buried wide
Now rest in safe Fricourt.

Endless rows of metal crosses,
Black against the August sun,
Shadows line the grassy mosses
Growing soft on everyone.

They knew not the horror waiting.
They knew not their sudden end.
They knew not the evil hating
Or the carnage round the bend.

Simon Matthews. libranstealphotography.co.uk

Simon Matthews. libranstealphotography.co.uk

Simon Matthews. libranstealphotography.co.uk

Butte de Warlancourt

This mound of earth
On which some trees
And bushes grow
Marks just the point
At which to show
The line where months
Of anguish sank
Into the bleeding heart
Of Picardy.

Here and at Thiepval
And Beaumont Hamel
Stopped the battle
Of the Somme
With all the yards
Of four months fighting
Sinking in November mud.

But
At the Butte de Warlencourt
To show what there
Had been before
There lay amid the nettle bank
Two large and unexploded shells.

The rusting twins
That missed their mark.

Nick Matthews. *horizonimage*

Poem

August
1916
Young
Adventure

Army
Brother
Flag
Enlist

England
Train
Ship
France

Pave
East
Western
Front

Billet
Battalion
Battery
Blood

Trench
Mud
Rain
Mud

Over
Top
Machinegun
Dead

Thistle Dump
Simon Matthews. libranstealphotography.co.uk

High Wood
Simon Matthews. libranstealphotography.co.uk

The View to High Wood

By the cemetery
Called Caterpillar Valley
One can see High Wood,
The home to many dead;
Or one may look on Thistle Dump instead.

And to the East at Delville Wood
The grave stones try to show
Where thousands died
Or disappeared.
But if you should
Touch on the ridge between them.
There is seen
The stone which marks the place
Where rest the Anzac men.

So near, beside the road,
There lay the Iron Harvest.
Three ploughmen worked the land
To show again the tangled wreckage
Of the place
Where sons were slaughtered, killed again,
Then ravaged
In the nightmare burial
Of whole battalions of men.

I stepped upon the sea of
Rusted carnage in the saddened sun
To view the wave-furrowed earth
Lap gently to the distant
Shores of sad
High Wood.

Nick Matthews. *horizonimage*

Nick Matthews. *horizonimage*

Nick Matthews. *horizonimage*

Thiepval Memorial
Somme

So many names rest bright across the lightened walls
That show the thousands dead across the Somme.
Look wide to find the units that they joined
And see the total slaughter of those groups
That stood for moments in the face of death.

Just finished on the slopes of neat High Wood
With nothing there to shelter them
And if they should, jump in a dull shell hole,
The mortar bombs would kill them,- whole.
And number up their names for all these years.

We look for Granddads, Uncles Great,
And take our time and always wait, and hope,
That here he did not die. But sure we see
The stark engravings of his death and loss
So long ago … and yet just yesterday.

Thiepval will arch our long and heartfelt hopes
That all those young lost souls will stay with us,
And live in all our hearts, remembered long,
To show our little ones the song
That war does little good
And should stay wrong!

Photograph - Dave Batchelor